Jann Wenner

Jann Simon Wenner (conceived January 7, 1946) is an American magazine head honcho who is a prime supporter of the mainstream society magazine Drifter, and previous proprietor of Men's Diary magazine. He partook in the Free Discourse Development while going to the College of California, Berkeley. Wenner, with his tutor Ralph J. Gleason, helped to establish Drifter in 1967.

Later in his profession, Wenner helped to establish the Wild Lobby of Acclaim and established different distributions. As a distributer and media figure, he has confronted debate in regards to Corridor of Notoriety qualification bias, the breakdown of his relationship with gonzo columnist Tracker S. Thompson, and analysis that his magazine's audits were one-sided

Early life and career

Wenner was brought into the world in New York City, the child of Sim and Edward Wenner. He experienced childhood in a mainstream Jewish family.

His folks separated in 1958, and he and his sisters, Kate and Merlyn, were shipped off live-in schools. He finished his optional training at the Chadwick School in 1963 and proceeded to go to the College of California, Berkeley. Prior to exiting Berkeley in 1966, Wenner was dynamic in the Free Discourse Development and delivered the section "Something's Going on" in the understudy run paper, The Day to day Californian.

With the assistance of his tutor, San Francisco Annal jazz pundit Ralph J. Gleason, Wenner got some work at Bulwarks, a high-dissemination mud slinger, where Gleason was a contributing manager and Wenner dealt with the magazine's side project paper

Media industry

In 1967, Wenner and Gleason established Drifter magazine in San Francisco. To kick the magazine off, Wenner acquired $7,500 from relatives and from the group of his prospective spouse, Jane Schindelheim.

All through the 1970s and 1980s, Wenner assumed a fundamental part in advocating journalists like Tracker S. Thompson, Ben Fong-Torres, Paul Nelson, Greil Marcus, Dave Bog, Grover Lewis, Timothy Crouse, Timothy Ferris, Joe Klein, Cameron Crowe, Joe Eszterhas and P.J. O'Rourke. He likewise found picture taker Annie Leibovitz when she was a 21-year-old San Francisco Workmanship Organization understudy. A considerable lot of Wenner's proteges, like Crowe, acknowledge him for giving them their greatest breaks. Tom Wolfe perceived Wenner's impact in guaranteeing that his most memorable novel, The Huge fire of the Vanities, was finished, expressing "I was totally frozen with fear about making it happen and I chose to serialize it and the main proofreader adequately insane to do that was Jann."

In 1977, Drifter moved its headquarters from San Francisco to New York City. The magazine's flow dunked momentarily in the last part of the 1970s and mid 1980s as Drifter answered gradually in covering the rise of underground rock and again during the 1990s, when it lost ground to Turn and Blender in inclusion of hip bounce. Wenner employed previous FHM manager Ed Needham, who was then supplanted by Will Dana, to turn his leader magazine around, and by 2006, Drifter's course was at an unsurpassed high of 1.5 million duplicates sold each fortnight. In May 2006, Drifter distributed its 1000th release with a holographic, three dimensional cover demonstrated on The Beatles' Sgt. Pepper's Forlorn Hearts Club Band collection cover

Wenner has been engaged with the leading and composing of large numbers of the magazine's Drifter Meetings. His meeting subjects have included: Bill Clinton, Al Violence, John Kerry, and Barack Obama for the magazine during their political races and in November 2005 had a meeting with U2 rockstar Bono, which zeroed in on music and politics.Wenner's meeting with Bono got a Public Magazine Grant designation.

Drifter and Wenner are chronicled in three books, Gone Off the deep end and Back Again by Robert Sam Anson, Drifter: The Uncensored History, and Tacky Fingers:The Life and Seasons of Jann Wenner and Drifter Magazine by Joe Hagan. Previous Drifter columnist David Weir is dealing with a memoir, as is writer and Beat history specialist Lewis MacAdams. Robin Green's journal The Main Young lady covers the time she worked at Drifter.

Wenner established the magazine Outside in 1977; wherein William Randolph Hearst III and Jack Portage both worked for the magazine before Wenner sold it a year after the fact. He likewise momentarily dealt with the magazine Look and, in 1993, began the magazine Everyday Life. In 1985, he purchased an offer in Us Week after week, trailed by a joint acquisition of the magazine with The Walt Disney Organization the next year. The magazine made the progress from a month to month to a week after week in 2000.In August 2006, Wenner purchased out Disney's portion and presently claims 100 percent of the magazine. From 2004 to 2006, Wenner contributed roughly $63,000 to Majority rule competitors and liberal organizations.[

In September 2016, Publicizing Age revealed that Wenner was currently offering a 49% stake in Drifter to an organization from Singapore called BandLab Advances. The new financial backer would have no immediate association in the publication content of the magazine. In October 2016, Wenner began distributing Glixel, a computer games based site.

In September 2017, Wenner Media declared that the excess 51% of Drifter was available to be purchased. That offer was purchased by Penske Media Organization, who later procured the excess stake from BandLab.

Controversy

Wenner, who was made an individual from the Rowdy Corridor of Popularity Establishment in 1983, has persevered through contention during his profession as it connects with his contribution in the association. Fans and allies of a few specialists have put a lot of fault on Wenner for keeping them out of the Corridor of Popularity. They guarantee Wenner has campaigned to keep them from thought and selection to the Corridor in light of individual predisposition and an aversion for their music. One hit ponders have been chosen for the Corridor of Acclaim while groups with numerous times of diagram achievement (Styx, Outsider, Boston, REO Speedwagon, and so on) remain barred.

In June 2007, Monkees bassist Peter Tork affirmed to the New York Post that Wenner is barring the gathering:

[Wenner] "doesn't mind what the guidelines are and simply works how he sees fit. It is a maltreatment of force. I don't know whether The Monkees have a place in the Lobby of Distinction, however obviously we're not in that frame of mind of an individual impulse." Tork accepts Wenner could do without the way that The Monkees, who were initially given a role as entertainers for a television sitcom, didn't play their own instruments on their initial two records. "Jann appears to have taken it harder than every other person, and presently, after 40 years, everyone gets out, 'Whatever's the serious deal? Every other person gets it done.' No one cares currently aside from him. He feels his ethical judgment in 1967 and 1968 should serve in 2007.

Hunter S. Thompson was to provide Rolling Stone coverage for the 1976 presidential campaign that would appear in a book published by the magazine. Reportedly, as Thompson was waiting for a $75,000 advance check to arrive, he learned that Wenner canceled the endeavor without telling him.

Wenner then asked Thompson to travel to Vietnam to report on what appeared to be the closing of the Vietnam War. Thompson accepted and arrived with the country in chaos, just as the United States was preparing to evacuate and other journalists were scrambling to find transportation out of the region. While there, Thompson learned that Wenner had canceled this excursion as well, and Thompson found himself in Vietnam without health insurance or additional financial support. Thompson's story about the fall of Saigon would not be published in Rolling Stone until ten years later.

These two incidents severely strained the relationship between the author and the magazine, and Thompson contributed far less to the publication in later years

Wenner terminated rock pundit Jim DeRogatis in 1996 after DeRogatis distributed a negative survey for a collection by the then-well known band Hootie and the Blowfish. Wenner pulled DeRogatis' audit from the magazine. Inquired as to whether Wenner loved Hootie and the Blowfish, DeRogatis answered that Wenner "honestly loves any band that sells 8,000,000 records." Wenner terminated DeRogatis the following day.

In June 2017, Wenner cut attaches with Joe Hagan, the biographer he had charged to compose his life story, Tacky Fingers, calling the book Hagan created "profoundly defective and tacky, as opposed to significant". Hagan had been working intimately with Wenner on the book beginning around 2013, and Tacky Fingers was delivered in October 2017

In the late spring of 1967, in the wake of Drifter began, Wenner and Jane Schindelheim were hitched in a little Jewish service. Wenner and his significant other isolated in 1995, however Jane Wenner actually stays a VP of Wenner Media. She and Wenner have three children, Alexander Jann, Theodore "Theo" Simon, and Edward Augustus, known as Gus, head of Wenner Media's computerized tasks.

Starting around 1995, Wenner's homegrown accomplice has been Matt Nye, a style creator. Together, Wenner and Nye have three youngsters conceived by means of proxy moms, Noah and twins Jude and India Rose

Working with a little gathering of recognized record organization heads and music industry experts, Wenner helped to establish the Wild Corridor of Distinction Establishment in 1983.

Wenner delivered Boz Scaggs' self-named significant mark debut collection in 1969.

Wenner made a visitor "appearance" in the Wonder Comic Thrill seeker issue 100 of every 1973, in which he meets the superhuman, who is consequently persuaded to recall his beginnings (which he imparts to the perusers of the comic, yet not with Wenner.)

In 1985, he delivered and showed up as himself in the film Wonderful with Jamie Lee Curtis and John Travolta. He likewise had appearance jobs in Cameron Crowe's movies Jerry Maguire and Practically Well known.

In 1985, Wenner had a Drifter cover photo of Wear Johnson carefully altered to eliminate the handgun and holster from the Miami Bad habit star as a result of Wenner's resistance to handguns.

The American Culture of Magazine Editors enlisted Wenner into their Corridor of Popularity in 1997, making him the most youthful proofreader at any point drafted.

Amy Beam bludgeoned Wenner as "Drifter's most valiant pioneer" in her melody "Lucystoners" from her 2001 performance debut Stag, blaming him for oppressing ladies specialists for a "young men's club of rock."

In 2004, Wenner was drafted into the Rowdy Lobby of Acclaim in the Lifetime Accomplishment class.

In the fall of 2007, Wenner distributed an oral memoir of Tracker S. Thompson named Gonzo: The Existence of Tracker S. Thompson. Co-composed with Corey Seymour, this work follows the existence of Thompson as recounted through the tales of those nearest to him.

In Walk 2014, it was reported that the distributer Knopf had gained a history of Wenner by writer Joe Hagan for a seven-figure cost. Denoting the 50th commemoration of Drifter was distributed in 2017.

Jann Wenner is Publication Overseer of Wenner Media and the organizer behind Drifter.

From its commencement in 1967, Moving Stone turned into the voice of an age, and is quite possibly of the best and famous magazine in distributing history, with various honors including 15 Public Magazine Grants. Wenner's obligation to quality news-casting has continued To move Stone in the front of the well known discourse, both recording and molding the general outlook through conclusive music inclusion, provocative meetings, grant winning photography and sharp analytical and political revealing.

As of now, Drifter has developed into a multi-stage content brand with unparalleled access and authority, which contacts north of 60 million individuals each month.

All through his vocation, Wenner has exhibited an instinctive comprehension of the changing interests of his perusers. In 1977, he established Outside, America's most memorable contemporary open air magazine, selling the title two years after the fact to another distributer.

In 1985, Wenner bought Us magazine, and repositioned the month to month distribution as "Us The Diversion Magazine," a state of the art source, highlighting close superstar interviews with grant winning writers, and rich portfolios by regarded photographic artists. In 2000, Us was relaunched as a week after week, and immediately set up a good foundation for itself as a definitive expert in VIP news-casting. Wenner offered the brand to one more distributer in mid 2017.

Wenner sent off Men's Diary in 1992, focusing on dynamic men keen on sports, travel and experience. He offered the brand to one more distributer in 2017.

In April 1997, Wenner turned into the most youthful inductee throughout the entire existence of the American Culture of Magazine Editors Lobby of Distinction. In 1994, he was named Distributing Chief of the Year by Adweek, a main industry exchange distribution. In Walk 2004, Wenner was enlisted into the Wild Corridor of Popularity for lifetime accomplishment. In 2010, he got The Norman Mailer Place's Award for Lifetime Accomplishment in Magazine Distributing. In 2014, Wenner got the LennonOno Award for Harmony grant.

Notwithstanding his distributing work, Wenner dedicates himself to various significant causes. He is director of the Rowdy Lobby of Notoriety Establishment, Inc., a 30-year-old philanthropic association which praises craftsmen and music industry experts who have made huge commitments to shake and roll.

Wenner is the dad of six kids. He dwells in New York City.

In 1967 he and Ralph J. Gleason helped to establish Drifter magazine. At the point when Gleason kicked the bucket in 1975, Wenner took over as distributer, a position he actually holds.

Wenner and his two more youthful sisters, Kate and Merlin were shipped off life experience schools after his folks separated in 1958.

He was propelled by The Beatles and The Drifters. He was likewise an old buddy of John Lennon and remains companions with Mick Jagger.

Left his significant other for model-turned-style fashioner Matt Nye. Wenner and his significant other were isolated in 1995. Following a 43-year marriage, their separation was concluded on 12 October 2011. They had three youngsters, Alex (took on), Theo, and Gus Wenner (Edward Augustus).

Positioned #5 of 50 persuasive individuals in The new York Eyewitness' "The New Power Gays" article, June 2011.

While "Drifter" magazine was sent off in November 9, 1967, Beatle John Lennon made the main cover in an exposure still from Remark j'ai gagné la guerre (1967). The magazine cost a quarter.

Has been an individual from the Rowdy Lobby of Notoriety Establishment starting around 1983. As a part, he has gotten through debate as fans and allies of a few craftsmen have put a lot of fault on him for keeping them out of the Lobby of Popularity. They guarantee he has campaigned to keep them from thought and selection to the Lobby of Distinction in view of individual predisposition and an abhorrence for their music. Peter Tork has expressed that feels the explanation that The Monkees are not in that frame of mind of Acclaim is a direct result of Wenner.

Had a run in with Tracker S. Thompson after he dropped a report what gave off an impression of being the end of the Vietnam War, which left Thompson in Vietnam without health care coverage or extra monetary help. Thompson's tale about the fall of Saigon wouldn't be distributed until a decade after the fact.

After Jim DeRogatis distributed a negative survey for a collection by Hootie and the Blowfish, Wenner had the survey pulled. Inquired as to whether Wenner loved Hootie and the Blowfish, Derogatis answered that he "loves any band that sells 8,000,000 records." Wenner terminated Derogatis the following day.

Rolling Stone was established in San Francisco in 1967 by Jann Wenner, a previous understudy at the College of California at Berkeley, and Ralph Gleason, a jazz pundit for the San Francisco Narrative paper. The principal issue showed up on Nov. 9, 1967, with John Lennon on the cover. The magazine's makers expected Moving Stone to be a gauge of the creative preferences and political sensibilities of the understudy age. The magazine actually joined energy and impressive skill, utilizing both legitimate English and "road language." Some notable authors and writers, including Tracker S. Thompson, Cameron Crowe, Lester Bangs, and Greil Marcus, began their vocations with Drifter. As the magazine progressively came to characterize huge patterns and knowing desire for rock and popular music, appearances on its cover were desired by laid out as well as anticipated performers as seals of basic achievement. Alongside the Beatles, Weave Dylan, Madonna, and numerous different artists, Drifter's cover included critical entertainers, authors, and lawmakers, like Jack Nicholson, Susan Sontag, and Bill Clinton. With an end goal to improve its picture, the magazine moved its workplaces to New York City in 1977.

In May 2006 Drifter printed its 1,000th issue. Its prosperity during that time was because of its capacity to adjust to continually evolving melodic, political, and social environments. Issues of Drifter ordinarily incorporate music and film surveys, big name stories and photos, data on new specialists, style guidance, and articles on legislative issues. Drifter has affected mainstream society through its "unsurpassed most prominent" records, for example, the "500 Biggest Collections Ever" (gave in November 2003) and the "100 Biggest Artists Ever" (gave in November 2008).

Irecommended that Like a Drifter appeared to be a way for Wenner to wrest back control of his own story after an encounter where he was a lot of not in charge of it. "No," he said. "Well, the facts confirm that I had trusted Joe's book would be the definitive record" — Hagan contends that it is the legitimate record — "yet this isn't in no way a reaction. At the end of the day, this is the way that I understood, at long last, I'm the one that can perceive it best. Out of nowhere, had opportunity and energy to make it happen and needed to make it happen.... I needed to do what I needed to do, which was simply recount to my story my way. Also, I needed to speak the truth about the times, and what they implied, and about the age. I needed to precisely depict my thought process is a vital verifiable age in American life."

The explanation Wenner abruptly had this time to burn was on the grounds that he had surrendered control of Drifter to 1) Jay Penske, whose Penske Media Company currently possesses the distribution; and 2) Gus Wenner — Jann's most youthful of three children from his union with Jane Schindelheim — who is presently Moving Stone's Chief. This was the piece of the book I was generally keen on. Perusers will without a doubt devour every one of the in the background candy highlighting any semblance of Bono, Weave Dylan, Bruce Springsteen, Bette Midler, and endless different stars, in addition to media symbols like Annie Leibovitz and Tracker S. Thompson, which is all flawlessly exemplified in Maureen Dowd's new Sunday Styles highlight on Wenner — as are accounts of medications, heartfelt connections, cherished recollections, and the magnificence days of the magazine. In any case, I needed to discuss the disintegration of Wenner Media, which I took care of as it was shaking out progressively.

The main Wenner title to go was Us Week by week in Walk 2017, trailed by Men's Diary in June 2017. Both went to American Media Inc., the grocery store cloth meets-wellness mag distributer then run by Chief and Trump buddy David Pecker, who might before long play a featuring job, close by Trump and Michael Cohen, in the famous catch-and-kill embarrassment. "Star and the Public Enquirer, his sensationalist newspapers, had run silly assaults on Trump's rivals," Wenner writes in one of the last sections, reviewing a get-together with Pecker. "That is not all, David told me. He had been purchasing and afterward spiking stories from ladies who had been laying down with Trump. He was extremely express about Trump's information, endorsement, and support. I simply considered this David boasting about being agreeable with the president. I referenced it to Gus and overlooked it." (To eavesdrop at that lunch!)

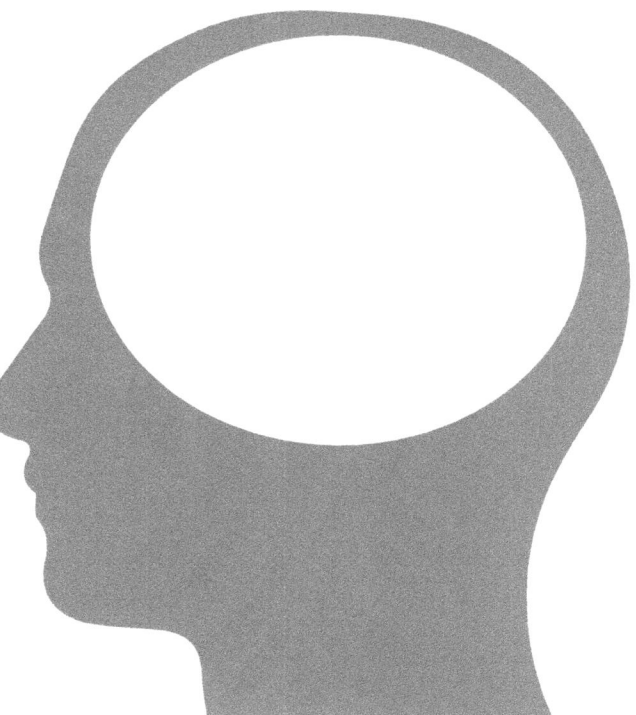

Milton Keynes UK
Ingram Content Group UK Ltd.
UKHW051507130923
428557UK00007B/74